Manitoba

Elizabeth Simon

WEIGL EDUCATIONAL PUBLISHERS

Published by Weigl Educational Publishers Limited
6325 10 Street SE
Calgary, Alberta, Canada
T2H 2Z9
Web site: www.weigl.com

We acknowledge the financial support of the Government of Canada through the Book Publishing
Industry Development Program (BPIDP) for our publishing activities.

National Library of Canada Cataloguing in Publication Data
Simon, Elizabeth
   Manitoba / Elizabeth Simon.
   (Canadian sites and symbols)
   Includes index.
   ISBN 1-55388-022-6
   1. Provincial emblems--Manitoba--Juvenile literature.
2. Heraldry--Manitoba--Juvenile literature. I. Title. II. Series.
CR213.M3S55 2003   j929.6'097127   C2003-910529-6

Printed in the United States of America
1 2 3 4 5 6 7 8 9 0   07 06 05 04 03

Project Coordinator: Heather C. Hudak
Design: Janine Vangool
Layout: Virginia Boulay
Copy Editor: Donald Wells
Photo Researcher: Barbara Hoffman

Photograph Credits
Every reasonable effort has been made to trace ownership and to obtain permission to reprint
copyright material. The publishers would be pleased to have any errors or omissions brought to
their attention so that they may be corrected in subsequent printings.

Cover: buffalo (Photos.com); **Barrett & MacKay:** page 18; **Corel Corporation:** pages 12, 13T, 15T;
CORBIS/MAGMA: page 4; **Doug Dealey Photographic Services:** pages 5, 7B, 11, 20; **Flin Flon and
District Chamber of Commerce:** page 7T; **Mike Grandmaison:** page 17; **Inco Ltd.:** page 16; **International
Peace Garden:** page 22; **Ray Joubert:** page 10; ©**Jon Kilimnik/JK Photography:** pages 3T, 6; **Keith
Levit Photography:** page 23; **Manitoba Culture, Heritage and Tourism/Archives of Manitoba:** page 19;
Bill Morgenstern/Earth Moods: page 14; **Photos.com:** page 9; **Province of Manitoba:** pages 1, 8; **Jim
Steinhart of www.Planetware.com:** page 21; **Travel Manitoba:** pages 3M, 3B, 13B, 15B.

Contents

Introduction

Canada is a large country. The ten Canadian provinces and three territories cover a vast amount of land. From one province or territory to another, the people, lifestyles, land, and animals are quite different. Each province and territory has its own **identity**. The provinces and territories use **symbols** to represent this identity. This book looks at the symbols that represent the province of Manitoba.

Wheat is Manitoba's most important crop.

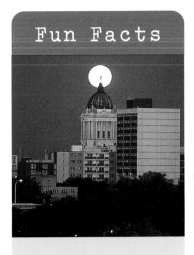

Manitoba is the most eastern of the three prairie provinces, which include Alberta and Saskatchewan. In the central and northern parts of Manitoba, there are dense forests, **tundra**, and about 100,000 lakes. Manitoba is in the centre of Canada, halfway between the Atlantic Ocean and the Pacific Ocean. Its central location, diverse landscapes, and history are represented by the province's official symbols.

Winnipeg is the capital of Manitoba. It is the oldest city in the prairie provinces.

More than 1 million people live in Manitoba.

About 16 percent of Manitoba's land is covered by lakes and large rivers. The largest lake in Manitoba is Lake Winnipeg. It is the thirteenth-largest lake in the world.

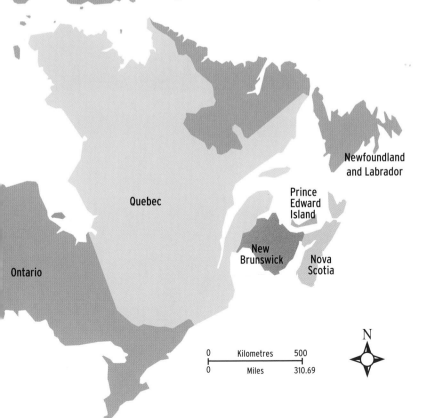

Ontario

Quebec

Newfoundland and Labrador

Prince Edward Island

New Brunswick

Nova Scotia

| 0 | Kilometres | 500 |
| 0 | Miles | 310.69 |

N

What's in a Name?

The name Manitoba comes from the Cree phrase *Manito bou*, which means "Narrows of the Great Spirit." Lake Manitoba narrows in the centre. At this place, the water laps against the shore and makes a wailing sound. The Cree believed the Great Spirit Manitou was part of everything in nature, including water. They believed the noise made by the waves was the sound of Manitou beating on a drum.

Lake Manitoba was once part of a larger lake called Lake Agassiz.

Manitoba is nicknamed the "Keystone Province." Keystones are stones or blocks that are used to hold up the sides of an arch. Manitoba is called the Keystone Province because it is the keystone in the arch of provinces that form Canada. Manitoba is also a keystone in Canada's communication, trade, and transportation industries.

Manitoba's southern region is a major contributor to Canada's breadbasket. Vast harvests of wheat, barley, oats, and flax come out of the region.

Fun Facts

The city of Flin Flon may have been named for Professor Josiah Flintabbatey Flonatin. Professor Flonatin is a character in a science fiction novel titled *The Sunless City* by E. Preston Muddock.

Manitoba is Canada's sixth-largest province.

About 35 percent of Manitoba is plains. Plains are a large area of flat, grassy land.

Coat of Arms Closeup

A coat of arms is a special design that stands for a group or a region. Each province and territory has its own coat of arms. Manitoba's coat of arms honours the history, land, and people of the province. Each symbol represents a different part of life in the Keystone Province.

GLORIOSUS · ET · LIBER

Fun Facts

The beaver is an important symbol of the early fur trade in Manitoba.

King Edward VII granted Manitoba its coat of arms on May 10, 1905.

Features

The crown represents Manitoba's role as a key province and its heritage as part of the British monarchy. The beaver is a symbol of Canada.

The prairie crocus held by the beaver is Manitoba's official flower.

The red and white wreath beneath the beaver represents Canada. Red and white are the official colours of Canada.

A unicorn and a horse stand on either side of the shield. The unicorn represents Manitoba's early Scottish settlers. The horse is an important animal to the culture of the Native Peoples, the Métis, and the European settlers.

The unicorn, horse, and shield stand on a base of water, grain fields, and forests.

Manitoba's Latin motto, *Gloriosus et Liber*, which means "Glorious and Free," is written on a ribbon that wraps around the base of the coat of arms.

Flying the Flag

Although Manitoba joined **Confederation** in 1870, it did not have an official provincial flag until 1965. Until then, the province used the Royal Union Flag, or Union Jack, as its official flag. The Union Jack is the flag of Great Britain. In 1964, the provincial government decided to design its own flag based on the Red Ensign. The Red Ensign was the flag of Canada. The Canadian Red Ensign was a red flag with the Union Jack in the upper corner. A shield made from portions of the New Brunswick, Nova Scotia, Ontario, and Quebec coats of arms was also on the Red Ensign.

Manitoba's flag has a red background. Red is a symbol of both Canada and Great Britain. The Union Jack is featured on the top left corner of the flag. Manitoba's shield is on the right side of the flag. Manitoba's flag was approved by Queen Elizabeth II in October 1965. It was officially adopted on May 12, 1966.

Fun Facts

Ontario also based its provincial flag on the Red Ensign.

The buffalo appears on Manitoba's shield. Native Peoples hunted buffalo for survival.

The Forks is Winnipeg's most popular tourist attraction. The Forks is built on the junction of the Assiniboine and Red Rivers. People have gathered at the Forks for more than 6,000 years.

Owls and Other Animals

Bison once roamed Manitoba's prairies. Today, most bison live in national parks because large parts of Manitoba's prairies have been turned into farmland. The bison is an important symbol of Manitoba's heritage. Coyotes, gophers, and rabbits are some of the animals that still live on the prairies. Beavers, black bears, deer, and moose make their homes in Manitoba's forests. Caribou, mink, and wolves survive in the cold, harsh climate of the tundra. Manitoba's many lakes and rivers are home to fish such as pike and trout.

Before the 1700s, Native Peoples followed and hunted bison herds on foot.

The great gray owl is the largest owl in North America. Males have wingspans up to 1.3 metres (4.3 feet) across. They fly close to the ground, usually no higher than 6 metres (20 feet) high. The great gray owl was named Manitoba's official bird in 1987. These owls live in Manitoba's northern, southern, and western forests.

Owls prefer to hunt at night. In northern Manitoba, it stays light much of the time, so the great gray owl must hunt during the day.

Fun Facts

Polar bears live near the northern Manitoba town of Churchill. This town has been called "The Polar Bear Capital of the World."

Winnie the Pooh was named after a real bear. A soldier from Winnipeg named Harry Colebourn owned the bear. He named it after his hometown. When a boy named Christopher Robin saw the bear, he named his stuffed teddy bear Winnie. Christopher's father, A. A. Milne, wrote a series of books about his son and Winnie the Pooh.

Tall Trees and Prairie Plants

F ew trees grow on Manitoba's prairies and tundra. Still, there are many areas where dense forests of birch, elm, oak, pine, and poplar trees grow. The white spruce became Manitoba's official tree in 1991. White spruce trees grow throughout the province. They usually live for about 200 years, but some live as long as 300 years. White spruce trees are important to Manitoba's logging industry.

Forests cover 40 percent of Manitoba. White spruce trees are found in the province's boreal forest.

Other plants and wildflowers also grow in Manitoba. In the tundra region, certain species of moss grow. The official flower of Manitoba is the prairie crocus. The prairie crocus is a purple flower with a furry stem. The flower was named by early settlers who saw them growing in the prairie region.

The prairie crocus was named Manitoba's floral emblem on March 16, 1906. It was chosen by schoolchildren.

Fun Facts

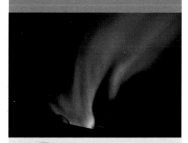

The Tundra Aurora Domes, located near Churchill, are areas with full views of the Northern Lights.

Sometimes, prairie crocuses begin to grow before the snow melts in the spring.

The white spruce is resistant to disease.

Native Peoples used the prairie crocus to treat muscle pain, nosebleeds, and cuts. They used the white spruce to make bowls, pots, and snowshoes.

Emblems of the Earth

Manitoba is rich in natural resources. Part of Manitoba lies on the **Canadian Shield**, which contains many minerals. Some of the minerals mined in Manitoba are copper, nickel, and zinc. Manitoba does not have an official mineral, but nickel is an important symbol of the province. Nickel is mined and produced in the northern city of Thompson. A company located in Thompson is the world's second-largest producer of nickel.

Thompson is home to one of the world's leading smelters. A smelter is a machine or factory that melts metal.

Nickel was once used to make Canada's five-cent coin. After World War I, the Royal Canadian Mint changed the amount of nickel used to make five-cent coins. Today, nickels are made mostly of steel. These five-cent coins are only 2 percent nickel. All Canadian **circulation** coins are made at the Royal Canadian Mint in Winnipeg.

Today, nickel is combined with other metals to make household items and appliances.

The first Royal Canadian Mint was located in Ottawa. In 1975, the Mint moved to Winnipeg. Since then, it has produced billions of coins for Canada and other countries around the world.

Many construction materials, such as cement, gravel, and sand, are found in Manitoba.

The Royal Canadian Mint produces an average of two billion coins each year.

A Symbolic Staff

Manitoba's legislature has an official mace. A mace is an ornamental stick that is carried as a symbol of authority. It represents the power of the province's government. The sergeant at arms places the mace on the table at the beginning of each session. The mace of Manitoba celebrates the **heritage** of the province's people. It has many interesting parts.

The Legislative Building of Manitoba is located in Winnipeg. People can watch sessions of the Legislative Assembly from the Visitors' Gallery.

Features

The top of the mace is a crown, which represents Canada's past as a colony of Great Britain.

Beavers sit on each of the four arches of the crown. The beaver is a symbol of Canada.

Below the crown is a cup that is divided into four parts. Each part is engraved with the symbol of one of the four founding countries of Canada. A rose represents England, a thistle represents Scotland, a shamrock represents Ireland, and a fleur-de-lis represents France.

An orb and cross are engraved on the mace. These symbols represent Manitoba's religious history. The mace weighs 13 kilograms (28 pounds).

Fun Facts

Manitoba's first mace was made from wood. The head was carved from a Red River cartwheel used during the Red River **Rebellion** in 1870. A Red River cart was a large wooden cart with two wheels that was used to carry meat and belongings to and from buffalo hunts. The staff was made from a flagstaff used during the same rebellion. This mace was used from 1871 to 1884.

Special Places

Every province and territory has at least one special place that represents its heritage. This place can be a historic fort, a monument, or a park. Manitoba has hundreds of heritage sites and two national parks. Two places that are very important to Manitoba's heritage are Riding Mountain National Park and Lower Fort Garry.

Riding Mountain National Park is located between Brandon and Dauphin in southwest Manitoba. This park represents Manitoba's many different landscapes. The park has **boreal** and **deciduous** forests, grasslands, and marshes. This park has an important history. It has been home to many of Manitoba's Native Peoples, such as the Ojibway and Assiniboine.

Riding Mountain National Park provides many recreational opportunities, such as camping, cross-country skiing, and hiking.

Lower Fort Garry is located in southern Manitoba near Winnipeg. It is a restored fort that was built by the Hudson's Bay Company. The Hudson's Bay Company was a British fur-trading company. It set up its first trading post in the Hudson Bay area. Over time, the trading company gained control of much of the land in the northwest of Canada. Lower Fort Garry was a major centre for trade and business. It is an important symbol of the history of Manitoba and the fur trade.

Actors recreate life in the 1800s at Lower Fort Garry. Visitors can tour historic buildings and learn about life at an 1850s fur-trading fort.

Fun Facts

The land owned by the Hudson's Bay Company was bought by the Canadian government in 1869. This included the land now known as Manitoba.

Riding Mountain National Park is home to animals such as bison, elk, and moose. It also has many birds. Some animals, such as cougars and wolves, are protected by law because they are in danger of becoming **extinct**.

Quiz

Based on what you have read, see if you can answer the following questions:

1.   What is the capital of Manitoba?

2.   Which company originally owned Lower Fort Garry?

3.   What animals appear on Manitoba's coat of arms?

4.   What is Manitoba's official tree?

The International Peace Gardens is located on the border of Manitoba and North Dakota in the United States. It is one of the greatest symbols of peace in the world.

5. What Manitoba town is sometimes called the "Polar Bear Capital of the World?"

6. What important mineral is used to make the Canadian five-cent coin?

7. What four countries are represented on Manitoba's official mace?

8. What is Manitoba's nickname?

Answers

8. The Keystone Province

7. England, Scotland, Ireland, and France

6. Nickel

5. Churchill

4. White spruce

3. Beaver, unicorn, and horse

2. Hudson's Bay Company

1. Winnipeg

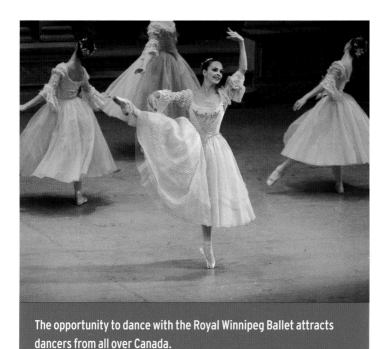

The opportunity to dance with the Royal Winnipeg Ballet attracts dancers from all over Canada.

Glossary

boreal: of the North or the Arctic

Canadian Shield: an area of ancient rock that covers part of Canada

circulation: the movement of something from place to place

Confederation: the joining of the Canadian provinces to form one country

deciduous: forests filled with trees that lose their leaves in autumn

extinct: no longer exists anywhere on Earth

heritage: past traditions, or something handed down from earlier generations

identity: the qualities that make one person or thing different from all others

rebellion: a violent action against the political system

symbols: things that stand for something else

tundra: a large, treeless plain in the Arctic

Index